W9-AUM-339

Inventions That Shaped the World

THE RAILROAD

JOHN R. MATTHEWS

Franklin Watts
A Division of Scholastic Inc.
New York · Toronto · London · Auckland · Sydney
Mexico City · New Delhi · Hong Kong
Danbury, Connecticut

Photographs © 2005: AP/Wide World Photos/Eugene Hoshiko: 66; Corbis Images: cover top, 11, 25, 40, 52, 59, 61 (Bettmann), cover bottom left, chapter openers (Colin Garratt/Milepost 92 1/2), 30 (E. O. Hoppé), 39 (Hulton-Deutsch Collection), 62 (Wolfgang Kaehler), 69 (James Leynse), timeline center (Arthur W.V. Mace/Milepost 92 $1/2$), timeline bubbles (Gordon Osmundson), 16 (Frances F. Palmer/Museum of the City New York), 42 (Underwood & Underwood) 18, 57; Getty Images: 27, 46 (Hulton Archive), 12 (Kean Collection/Hulton Archive), cover bottom right (The Bridgeman Art Library); Mary Evans Picture Library: 32 (Douglas McCarthy), 24; Masterfile: 6 (David Mendelsohn), 64 (Ron Stroud); North Wind Picture Archives: 15, 49 (Nancy Carter), 9, 50, 54; Photo Researchers, NY/SIBL/New York Public Library: 28; The Image Works: 21 (HIP/Science Museum, London), 22 (NRM/Cuneo Fine Arts/SSPL), 37 (NRM/SSPL), 33 (SSPL).

Cover design by The Design Lab
Book production by The Design Lab

Library of Congress Cataloging-in-Publication Data
Matthews, John R., 1937–
  The railroad / John R. Matthews.
    p. cm. — (Inventions that shaped the world)
  Includes bibliographical references and index.
  ISBN 0-531-12372-3 (lib. bdg.)   0-531-16745-3 (pbk.)
  1. Railroads—Juvenile literature. I. Title. II. Series.
  TF148.M38 2005
  385—dc22
                                       2004030269

Contents

CHAPTER ONE

The Coming of the Railroad

You probably hear a train whistle sometimes. Do you wonder where that train came from or where it is going? If it is a freight train, how many different railcars does it have? Perhaps it is pulling tanker cars carrying gasoline from a refinery. Some cars may be shipping containers headed for an inland freight terminal. You might see hopper cars, or freight-train cars that have floors that slope toward doors for unloading material, carrying coal to an electricity-generating plant. Perhaps it is a passenger train. Is it a *commuter train* that carries people to work in the morning and home at the end of the day? Perhaps it is a long-distance train that goes from city to city. Does it have a dining car? Can passengers spend the night in individual sleeping compartments?

A freight train carries lumber for delivery. Different trains have different purposes. There are commuter trains, long-distance trains, and freight trains.

Trains travel on railroads. Railroads are one way for people to travel around the country. Trains are also important for moving freight from one place to another. Freight is anything that is carried on trucks, ships, or trains. The lumber or bricks used to build your home may have been brought to your town by train. Many things you see in stores were carried in trains to freight terminals to be loaded onto trucks for local delivery.

If you look at a map of the United States showing all the railroads, you will see railroad tracks covering the entire country. Both freight and passenger trains use the same tracks. Passenger trains stop at passenger stations to pick up and let off riders. Some bigger cities have large and elaborate train stations. Most of these train stations were built in the late nineteenth or early twentieth centuries. Then, trains were the favorite way for people to travel from one city to another or to travel across the country. Once air travel became popular in the middle of the twentieth century, long-distance train travel diminished. When the interstate highway system was built, also in the middle of the twentieth century, train travel diminished even further. Many people preferred to travel long distances by plane. They preferred to drive or take buses to travel short distances.

Passenger Trains

Even though passenger service has declined, it is still possible to travel by train. Long-distance train passengers travel up and down the East Coast or across the country. People who live outside large cities, such as New York or Boston, can go to and from the city center in commuter trains.

There are other kinds of passenger trains besides commuter trains and those that travel from city to city. Large cities once had *streetcars,* which were electric trains that ran on tracks in the middle of city streets. Streetcars were slow, so some cities built *subways,* which are underground trains. Railroad tracks were placed underground so that

7

trains could travel very fast and not interfere with pedestrian and automobile traffic on the streets. Because these subways could travel fast, they became known as *rapid-transit systems.*

Some cities built rapid-transit systems called *light rails.* These systems are similar to subways, except that most travel on the surface rather than underground. Some light rails may be elevated above streets, where they can travel without interference from street traffic, just like subways.

A Wonderful Idea

Life would be less pleasant without railroads. Although air travel has taken passengers away from long-distance trains, planes are not suitable for short commuter travel between suburbs and cities. Although automobile travel is increasing, cars are not a good substitute for rapid-transit systems in cities because parking places are scarce and expensive.

How did the idea for railroads come about? Like many other wonderful inventions, the railroad was invented in the early nineteenth century during the Industrial Revolution. That was a time when machines were being invented to replace human laborers. The new machines, powered by steam from boiling water, needed vast quantities of coal to fuel their engines. Horse-drawn wagons had a hard time delivering all the necessary coal. Factories

The railroad was invented in the early 1800s during the Industrial Revolution. Horsedrawn wagons could not deliver the amount of goods that were being manufactured.

also produced many more goods. There was no efficient way to get those goods from the factories to the people who wanted to buy them. Wagons, carts, and river barges adequately transported goods produced in home workshops. But with the increase in factory-made goods, a better transport system was needed. The railroad would be the solution.

Inventing the Railroad

Parts of the railroad system were already invented and in

use in the early nineteenth century. Primitive wooden rails were already used for guiding coal or ore carts out of mines. Steam engines were already used for pumping water out of mines and running factory machines. The railroad inventor's role was to put the parts together and invent something completely new.

Several inventors saw the possibility for developing the railroad. In 1803, Englishman Richard Trevithick was hired by Samuel Homfray to build a *locomotive* for his iron works. Trevithick then built the first locomotive to run successfully on rails. He called his engine a locomotive because the word means "to move from one place to another." The engine worked, but it was not considered practical and was not developed after its first demonstration. Trevithick kept building better and better locomotives. He finally demonstrated that locomotives could someday pull cars carrying passengers and freight.

Two inventors who developed a practical locomotive for a railway were Englishmen George Stephenson and his son Robert. Although others before them had built engines and even railways, it was the Stephensons who demonstrated that the railroad could become a successful transport system. Over time, other inventors added improvements, but it is Richard Trevithick and the Stephensons who can be called the railroad's inventors.

CHAPTER TWO

Transportation Before the Railroad Era

Before railroads were built in the early nineteenth century, moving goods from one place to another was difficult and slow. Ships brought manufactured goods from factories in Europe to U.S. ports such as New York and Boston. Other ships might bring the same goods to ports farther south such as Charleston, South Carolina, or Savannah, Georgia. Some of the goods had to be

Ships delivered goods from Europe and other continents to the United States.

Goods shipped from Europe had to be transported inland so they could be sold. Many of the goods were put onto barges to be transported to their final destinations.

moved inland to stores where they would be sold. From New York, goods could be moved up the Hudson River and through the Erie Canal on barges. Ships and barges were slow. A barge might average 5 miles (8 kilometers) per hour while early trains could travel at 35 miles (56 km) per hour. Because of its greater speed, the railroad made the shipment of perishable goods such as fresh vegetables and other foodstuffs possible.

Transporting Freight: Waterways

If you look at a map of the United States, you can see that most older cities are located near a river, seacoast, or one of the Great Lakes. That is because before railroads strectched across the United States, waterways were the best way to travel and to transport goods.

The most popular sites for cities were alongside larger rivers that could accommodate big boats and barges. For example, Saint Louis, Missouri, is located where the Missouri and Mississippi rivers meet. Its location provides easy access to many other cities on waterways, such as Minneapolis, Minnesota, and Memphis, Tennessee. It also has access to the seaport at New Orleans, Louisiana.

Other cities are located near one of the Great Lakes. Chicago, Detroit, and Buffalo are examples. When railroads began to spread in the middle of the nineteenth century, these and other cities would become important destinations for them.

Some rivers or sections of rivers were not deep enough for boats or barges to pass. Some of these were canalized to provide transportation to other cities. Canalizing a river means building dams and locks or dredging shallow parts of the river. Dams raised the water level so boats and barges could float. Locks are enclosures in a canal with gates at each end used to raise and lower boats as they pass through waterways with different water levels.

The Erie Canal

The 363-mile (584-km) long Erie Canal, which was built in stages, finally broke through to Lake Erie in 1825. That year the first canal boat made the trip from Lake Erie to New York City, beginning on October 26. The canal was 4 feet (1.2 meters) deep and 40 feet (12 m) wide. It was later enlarged to a depth of 7 feet (2.1 m). While it was being built, it was often mockingly referred to as Clinton's Ditch or Clinton's Folly. DeWitt Clinton was the governor of New York who championed the construction of the canal and pushed it to completion.

The canal connected Lake Erie to the Hudson River. It opened water traffic from New York City to the Great Lakes. It made New York the busiest seaport in the United States and opened the Great Lakes Region to rapid settlement.

Transporting Freight: Wagons

Once freight had been delivered to seacoast or river ports, it had to be distributed inland. Manufactured goods had to be brought to stores. Supplies such as lumber and bricks had to be delivered to building sites. Before railroads, the only way to transport freight over land was in wagons.

The most popular freight wagon was the *Conestoga wagon.* The Conestoga wagon was a large, four-wheeled wagon usually pulled by six horses or four oxen. German settlers in Pennsylvania first used this kind of wagon, which was named after the Conestoga Valley in which they lived. It had a large, fabric hood to protect its cargo

When freight arrived by ship, covered wagons would transport it over land. The most popular freight wagon was the Conestoga wagon pictured here.

from rain or snow. It could haul about 6 tons of freight. The wagon body was usually waterproof so that it could float like a barge when the wagon wheels were removed. Because wagons were so slow and cumbersome, railroads quickly replaced them for long-distance transport.

Transporting Passengers: Ships and Waterways

Before the coming of the railroad, passengers up and down the East Coast of the United States could travel in ships that hugged the coast, away from the perils of the open ocean. On the larger rivers, such as the Missouri, the Ohio, and the Mississippi, passengers could travel in paddle-wheel steamers. The writer Mark Twain wrote stories about travel on Mississippi riverboats. Some boats were as elaborate as oceangoing steamboats and featured live entertainment.

Once passengers reached the port nearest their destination, they had to transfer to other transportation modes. Their choices depended on how far they had to travel and which vehicles were available.

Passengers wanting to travel on the largest rivers could ride on paddle-wheeled streamers. Some were very fancy and featured live entertainment.

Transporting Passengers: Horses, Buggies, Coaches, and Wagons

Horseback was one way to travel. The advantage was that horses could move over rough terrain that vehicles could not. The disadvantages were that you couldn't carry much luggage or more that one companion. Buggies were family vehicles, usually drawn by one or two horses and useful for local travel. Coaches were commercial vehicles drawn by four or six horses that traveled from town to town. Wagons were useful when moving an entire family. Many people walked from one town to another. They often traveled as fast as coaches.

Railroads were not extended into the western states and territories until the middle and late nineteenth century. Before that, settlers traveling from eastern states to western territories moved their families and their belongings in wagons. They used wagons called *prairie schooners,* which were similar to Conestoga wagons. They were called schooners because the white canvas coverings were made from sailcloth that was similar to the material used used for schooner-ship sails. Prairie schooners were lighter than Conestoga wagons and needed only two or four horses to pull them. Families migrating in prairie schooners usually traveled in convoys referred to as *wagon trains*. Groups traveling together provided mutual help and security. Once a family reached its destination, the horseshoe-shaped covering was removed from the prairie schooner, and the schooner became a farm wagon. When railroads reached the western territories in the late nineteenth century, settlers and other travelers quickly switched from wagon trains to railroad trains.

The Railroad

Many people contributed to the development of the railroad, but three inventors—Richard Trevithick and George and Robert Stephenson—were especially important. They invented the steam locomotives that made modern railroads possible. In 1825, the Stephensons showed how locomotives could replace horse-drawn wagons on the first railway, which connected Darlington with Stockton in England.

Wagon trains were used for families or groups that were moving from one town to another. Often wagon trains traveled through mountainous terrain.

CHAPTER THREE

The Locomotive Inventors

The railroad was developed in stages over a long period. The idea for railroad tracks was inspired by the wooden rails used to guide wagons carrying coal and ore out of mines. The steam engine, the most important part of the first railroad locomotives, was already widely used to pump water from mines by the time the locomotive was invented.

Richard Trevithick

Born in 1771 in Cornwall, England, Richard Trevithick was born to a mining family. As a teenager Trevithick went to work with his father at the mines. He soon became an apprentice *engineer.* Engineers were people who knew how to make and repair engines. Today, they would be called mechanics.

Trevithick learned by doing. As he learned the engineering trade he began to attract attention by making improvements to the mine's steam engine, and he was promoted to engineer. He developed a better engine for raising ore out of the mine, and it was soon in great demand. He also began experiments to develop a steam locomotive.

Newcomen's Engine

The steam engines used in the mines where Trevithick worked were developed in the early eighteenth century by Thomas Newcomen. They were later improved by James Watt. These were very primitive, low-powered engines. Both Newcomen's and Watt's engines were called "atmospheric engines" because they used the opposing forces of air (atmospheric pressure) and a *vacuum* to operate their pumps.

By 1796, Trevithick had produced a successful locomotive, but it was just a miniature model. He next tackled a full-sized locomotive. By Christmas Eve 1801, he was ready to demonstrate it. He took seven friends on a short ride in the locomotive. It traveled only a few hundred feet before it lost steam and stopped. Trevithick named the engine Puffing Devil, or Puffer, because of the noise it made. Puffing Devil was built to run on roads rather than on railroad tracks.

Trevithick's Engines

In 1803, Richard Trevithick was hired by Samuel Homfray, owner of the Penydarren Ironworks, to develop a steam-powered vehicle. Homfray wanted a vehicle to pull wagons full of iron from his factory to a nearby canal. A year later, in 1804, Trevithick demonstrated the first steam locomotive, the Penydarren, to run successfully on rails. Like the Puffer, the Penydarren consisted of one cylinder, which is a metal sleeve. The cylinder stood upright on the engine. Inside the

Richard Trevithick built the first steam locomotive.

cylinder was a piston, or plunger. The piston was connected to a large wheel by a rod. When the steam pressure moved the piston, the piston turned the large wheel, which, in turn, turned the locomotive's wheels.

On its first journey, this engine pulled a train of five wagons loaded with 10 tons (9 metric tons) of iron and seventy passengers. The Penydarren made only three trips. At 7 tons (6.3 metric tons), the engine was too

The locomotive Penydarren was demonstrated for the first time in 1804. It pulled both passengers and five wagons loaded with iron.

heavy for the tracks, and the cast-iron rails frequently broke. Rails were made by casting, or pouring, molten iron into molds. The result was very brittle rails that broke easily. Later, rails would be made of steel, a stronger alloy consisting of several different metals, including iron. Homfray concluded that using a locomotive that damaged the railway tracks was not a good way to transport his iron, and he abandoned the project.

In 1808, Trevithick built another locomotive, which he named Catch-me-who-can. This locomotive ran on a circular track enclosed by a high wooden fence. Visitors were charged admission to the enclosure to ride behind the locomotive as it was driven around the track. Shortly after this

Trevithick's Cornish Boiler

Steam-engine boilers were large, horizontal cylinders for boiling water to make steam. Heat to boil the water came from a coal-burning firebox beneath the boiler. In 1812, Trevithick made a major improvement in the steam engine with a new design for the engine's boiler. This boiler was called the Cornish boiler.

Trevithick placed a tube inside the boiler to hold the burning coal. The burning coal in turn heated the water surrounding the tube. Trevithick's tube burned the coal more efficiently. The new boiler allowed the engine to do double or triple the work of previous engines with the same amount of coal.

One of Trevithick's inventions, the Catch-me-who-can engine was the center-piece at the steam circus in London.

amusement ride was established, the locomotive broke the rails. Trevithick lost interest in the project and abandoned it.

Trevithick became bankrupt in 1811, but he continued to make improvements to steam engines. Between 1816 and 1827, he worked in South America. First, he supervised the installation of pumping engines in gold and silver mines in Peru. Then, in 1822, he moved on to the copper mines of Costa Rica and Colombia before returning home to England in 1827.

Even though Trevithick was a poor businessman and

often penniless, he was well-known and respected as an engineer and inventor. After his return from South America, however, he found that many of his former colleagues had forgotten him. Nevertheless, in 1832, he was hired to work on an experimental engine for a steamship. He worked on the project until his death in 1833. The Trevithick Society in England honors his work with an annual celebration at Camborne in Cornwall, England.

George Stephenson

George Stephenson was born in England in 1781 in a small village called Wylam. As a boy, he watched coal wagons pass along the banks of the river Tyne, which was near his home. The coal wagons were pulled by horses on *wagonways.* Wagonways were roads with wooden tracks that guided the wagons.

George Stephenson, inventor of the first practical railroad locomotive, learned engineering skills by working in coal mines as a teenager.

George Stephenson went to work while still a child. His first job was to herd cows that grazed along the road and keep them off the tram-road, or wagonway, and out of the way of the coal wagons. At about age fifteen, George went to work in the mines with his father. His job was to pick stones and rubble from the coal before it was sent out on the wagons. Soon after starting work, he was promoted to *fireman.*

Two years later, he was operating and maintaining the mines' engines. In his spare time, Stephenson learned as much as he could about the engines. He took them apart and put them back together again. Knowledge gained this way allowed him to quickly repair engines when they malfunctioned.

Stephenson had little formal education. He was nearing manhood before he learned to read. At eighteen, he was barely able to write his own name. In his late teens, he attended night school three nights a week. He learned reading and spelling. He attended another school to learn arithmetic. Because he worked full time in the mines, he struggled to find time to study.

Stephenson's First Locomotive

One day in 1813, Stephenson watched a steam engine pull a string of sixteen coal cars at a speed of about 3 miles (5 km) per hour. He was asked what he thought of it, and he replied that he "could make a better one than that." He began work on developing a better engine.

In 1814, Stephenson demonstrated his first steam locomotive, the Blucher. It could pull eight cars with a total

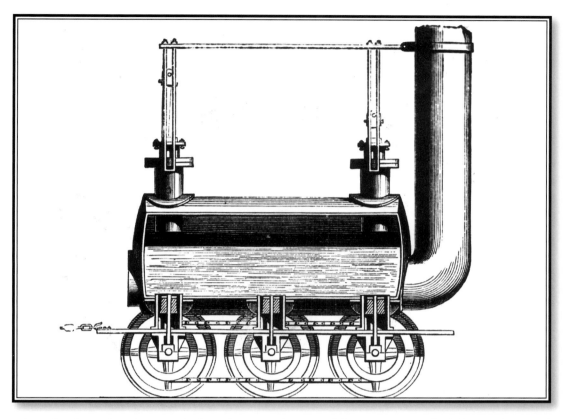

The Blucher, Stephenson's first locomotive, could carry more freight and travel at faster speeds than any other locomotive.

weight of 30 tons (27 metric tons) up a grade at 4 miles (6 km) per hour. In 1821, Stephenson demonstrated the Blucher to Edward Pease, who was building a horse-drawn railway from Darlington to Stockton, England. Pease was so impressed with Stephenson's locomotive that he hired him as chief engineer for the new railway, which opened in 1825. Pease then changed the railway from a horse-drawn to a locomotive railway.

This is an historical diagram of a steam locomotive by Stephenson. It was the first locomotive to have a steam-blast.

Stephenson's first engine took advantage of Trevithick's technological innovations. His 1814 engine had a cylindrical boiler, 8 feet (2.4 m) long and almost 3 feet (0.9 m) in diameter. He made one important improvement to this locomotive. He added a device he called a spur-gear, which increased the power of the locomotive.

Though the Blucher was successful, the engine had

trouble generating sufficient steam to keep it running. Stephenson accidentally hit upon the solution to that problem by discovering the *steam-blast.* The steam-blast was a pipe that captured the excess steam that would normally be discharged into the air and rerouted it to the smokestack. There it mixed with the exhaust from the burning fuel. It created a vacuum, which made the fire burn hotter, which in turn created more steam.

The Steam-blast

Stephenson's discovery of the steam-blast was accidental. When steam escaped from the steam pipe into the open air, it made a loud, puffing noise that frightened horses at road crossings. The horses' owners complained to the police. The police threatened to arrest Stephenson. Stephenson developed the steam-blast to eliminate the noise. Only later did he discover that the steam-blast also made his engine more efficient.

Stephenson Improves Locomotive Designs

Stephenson began to improve the Blucher in 1815. He used the knowledge he gained from the first design to make further improvements. One important improvement replaced his spur-gear, the device that transferred power from the engine to the wheels. After several experiments with attaching chains to the wheels, Stephenson developed a system of rods that connected all the wheels to the engine. This system is still in use. If you look at the wheels of a modern locomotive, you will see a horizontal rod connecting the front wheels to the rear wheels. When the train moves, you can see the rod move up and down, keeping all the wheels synchronized.

Another important innovation Stephenson added to his locomotives was a new wheel design. To keep the wheels from slipping off the tracks, he put a *flange,* or lip, on the inside edge of the wheels, which locked them firmly into place on the tracks.

In 1820, the Duke of Portland, who built the first rail-

Stephenson added flanges to the wheels to keep them from slipping off the tracks. The system of rods that connect all the wheels to the engine is still used today.

road in Scotland, ordered a locomotive from Stephenson. Like most of the locomotives at that time, it was to be used to transport coal. Stephenson named this engine the Duke. It had six wheels instead of the usual four. The wheels were driven by connecting rods, as they were on Stephenson's previous engine. This engine was not successful because its weight tended to damage the tracks. It could only haul 10 tons (9 metric tons) at 5 miles (8 km) per hour. That was not much better than a team of horses could do, so it was abandoned.

In 1826, planning began for the Liverpool to Manchester railway in England, and Stephenson was hired as the engineer. The majority of the railway's directors wanted the railway cars to be drawn by horses. Others wanted to place stationary engines at intervals along the tracks. The trains would be drawn by chains or cables from one stationary engine to the next, like present-day cable cars.

George Stephenson, who had been hired by the railway company to supervise the project, favored using locomotives instead of stationary engines or horses. Stephenson's vision of railway trains pulled by locomotives prevailed.

A prize of 500 English pounds was offered to the person who could design the best locomotive to run on the new railway. The Rocket, designed by Stephenson's son Robert was chosen. Its performance was by far the best, and it did not damage the tracks. During the trial, the Rocket reached a top speed of 29 miles (47 km) per hour. That was nearly three times the speed the judges expected. The Rocket was regarded as the first truly successful steam locomotive. The Liverpool to Manchester railroad opened in 1830.

The Rocket demonstrated that railroads were a viable mode of transportation. Locomotives were destined to become the dominant method for carrying both freight and passengers. George Stephenson and his son Robert continued to develop railway technology in England throughout their lives.

The Rocket paved the way for locomotives to become the preferred method of shipping freight and passengers.

Inventing the Railroad

The railroad is a complex transportation system that was developed over many years. Each piece of the system is an important part of the whole. First, there were the wooden tracks of the wagonways. Then, iron strips were added to the tracks. Then came the first locomotives. Eventually, small improvements added up to make a workable railway system. Inventors

The railroad system as we know today took many years to develop.

improved existing technologies to produce something entirely new. Richard Trevithick improved James Watt's steam engine and used it to invent the first locomotive. George and Robert Stephenson improved Trevithick's locomotive and used it to invent the transportation system recognizable as the first railroad.

Need, as well as existing technology, also plays a role in inspiring invention. After all, it was a businessman, Samuel Homfray, who asked Trevithick to build a locomotive. He needed a better way to transport iron and coal than the horse-drawn railways then in use. Industrial growth also created a need for better transportation.

In eighteenth- and nineteenth-century England, large

Wagonways

Tracks, or rails, were in use long before the invention of the railroad. Wooden railways were used in central European mines as early as the sixteenth century. The first wooden railway in England was built in 1604. Iron strips were fastened to the wooden rails to add strength. The tracks guided the wagon wheels much as modern railroad tracks guide trains by keeping the wheels positioned properly.

These wagonways were built to run downhill from a mine to a river or harbor. Loaded wagons could coast downhill. Once unloaded, they were then pulled uphill back to the mine by horses.

machines in factories were replacing handwork and cottage industries. More mines were needed to provide iron for the machines and coal to fuel the steam engines. As the mines were dug deeper, water that accumulated at the bottom of them could no longer be pumped out by hand. Thomas Newcomen came to the rescue with a new invention in 1712. His steam engine could run the pumps that cleared the mines of water. James Watt improved on the steam engine by designing one of his own, which he patented in 1769. It was Watt's engine that inspired Richard Trevithick to invent his locomotive.

Newcomen's and Watt's engines created a vacuum. The vacuum could move the piston of a pump. To create the vacuum, steam in the engine's boiler was forced into a *condenser.* The steam forced out air. When the condenser was cooled, the steam inside was condensed back into water. The water volume was much less than the steam volume. The result was an empty, airless space, or vacuum, inside the condenser.

When Trevithick and later George Stephenson built steam engines that used steam pressure instead of vacuums, Watt denounced the practice as dangerous. Indeed, he was right. Engine boilers under high pressure sometimes exploded. Nevertheless, the high-pressure engines were so much more powerful and efficient that they soon replaced Watt's engines.

Trevithick's Steam Engines

James Watt's patent for his steam engine kept anyone from building one like it without his permission. Trevithick's desire to build an engine without violating Watt's patent rights inspired him to design a new type engine.

In 1798, Trevithick began work on a full-scale stationary engine. Once he believed this engine was powerful enough to propel itself, he began work on a self-propelled vehicle that could carry passengers. The result in 1801 was a steam vehicle, the Puffing Devil, made to travel on a street rather than on a railroad. He took several of his friends for a joy ride in the vehicle, but while they were stopped at a restaurant, Puffing Devil caught fire and burned. He made another in 1803 that ran several times in London before he turned his attention to railways.

Despite the problems, Trevithick had invented a successful steam locomotive. Someone else would have to develop a better railway track to make the railroad a viable invention. That inventor was George Stephenson, who made crucial changes that resulted in the first practical, long-distance locomotive.

George Stephenson's Railroad

Several engine makers attempted to improve Trevithick's locomotive before George Stephenson entered the contest. The Englishmen Matthew Murray and John

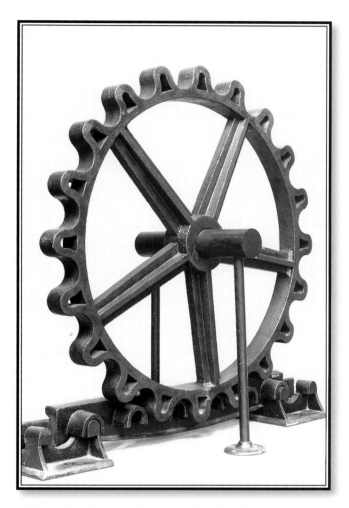

John Blenkinsop's cogged wheels were especially helpful on mountain railways.

Blenkinsop, his partner built several successful locomotives in 1812 and 1813. Their locomotives had cogged wheels that gripped a toothed rack rail, like the gears of a clock. Because of the expense of building rails suitable for these engines, they never became popular.

In 1813 or 1814, William Hedley, also an Englishman, built an experimental carriage that had eight wheels instead of four to spread out its weight on the rails. It was not a success. Hedley's own evaluation was that "It went badly; the obvious defect being want of steam." However, it did contribute to locomotive technology. It showed that locomotives with smooth wheels could grip the rails strongly enough to travel quickly. That eliminated the need for Murray's cogged-wheel and rack-rail system. Hedley's locomotive may have been the engine that inspired George Stephenson to remark, "I can build a better one."

By 1820, people began to realize that locomotives might have uses other than hauling coal and ore. They could be used for the general transport of both freight and passengers. Thomas Gray, an Englishman, spent much of his time and money publishing pamphlets advocating the use of locomotives for general transportation between Liverpool and Manchester and other points. He was so passionate on the subject that his friends thought him to be insane. Meanwhile, George Stephenson was embarking on just such an enterprise.

George Stephenson's Railroad

By 1820, Stephenson had a prosperous factory in Newcastle, England, for manufacturing locomotives. From there he designed and constructed the Darlington to Stockton railway line, the first passenger railroad. The railway was opened in September 1825. For the opening, he had three engines ready to be put into service. Crowds came from miles around to see the first departure. Stephenson drove the locomotive himself.

The engine Stephenson chose to drive that day was called

Passengers dressed up for the 1825 opening of the world's first steam traction, freight, and passenger railway.

the Locomotion. Crowds gathered to watch as the Locomotion departed. The Stephensons' success led to other locomotive sales, including to the Bolton and Leigh railway, and eventually to the Liverpool and Manchester railway.

Better Rails

The success of the locomotive forced track builders to solve the problem of frequently broken rails. Before the new locomotives could be used on railroads, the rails needed to be made more durable. Rails from the early nineteenth century made of iron plates were adequate for horse-drawn wagons but frequently broke under the greater weight of locomotives. The invention of the *T-rail,* a rail shaped like an upside-down capital T, strengthened the iron rails, but iron is brittle, and the iron rails still broke easily.

The solution was to make rails using steel, an alloy containing iron and other metals that is stronger than plain

Workers lay down steel rails which were more durable than iron. In 1869, a group of Irish rail-layers set a record by laying down 10 miles (16 km) of track in one day.

iron. Steel rails began replacing iron ones in the late 1800s, and by the early twentieth century, almost all the rails in the United States were made of steel. Rail weights have increased since the nineteenth century from about 40 to 80 pounds (18 to 36 kilograms) per linear yard to about 112 to 145 pounds (51 to 66 kg) per linear yard today. The heavier rails are used for high-speed lines and lines used to haul heavy loads.

Railway Signals and Switches

As railway traffic increased, a system was needed to prevent collisions between two trains on the same track. The next time you ride in a train, look out the window to see what appear to be traffic lights. These are signals that train operators depend on to tell them how to proceed. Early signals were not lights, but flag-shaped devices on poles. They were tripped by a lever operated by a signalman who knew whether or not the track ahead was occupied by another train.

Later, mechanical devices tripped a signal as a train passed a point at which other trains needed to be warned of its location. Now signals are electrically operated and are interlocked, meaning that they are prevented from sending conflicting signals. For example, if one signal tells a train to proceed, other interlocked signals automatically tell other trains to stop.

When additional rail lines were built, "switch men" were needed to divert trains onto other tracks.

Switches are part of the signal system and are used to divert one train onto a side track and out of the path of another train. Switches are also used when trains need to change from one rail line to another.

The first railroad was just a straight line from one town to another. As additional rail lines were built, switches were needed to move trains from one rail line to another. Switches are a pair of tapered rails running alongside each track that can divert a train onto another track when moved into position. Early switches were activated with a manually operated lever that moved the switch tracks. Today, switches are operated electrically.

Railroad Crossings

Places where railroads intersect with roads are called railroad crossings. Because trains need long distances to stop, road vehicles at crossings must always yield the right-of-way to trains. Safety procedures to prevent accidents have evolved since the railroads were constructed.

Early procedures involved stationing a worker at a busy intersection with a lantern to signal traffic to stop to let a train pass. Later, flashing red lights were installed at crossings to warn traffic that a train was coming. These warning lights are in use today and are usually accompanied by loud, clanging bells and sometimes a traffic arm that is lowered in the path of traffic.

Railway Tunnels

Trains cannot climb or descend steep inclines. Incline, called grade, is measured by the height the terrain rises while going up a hill. A 1-foot (0.3-m) rise every 100 feet (30 m) of track is called a 1 percent grade. Railroad builders don't like a grade greater than about 1.5 percent. When railroad tracks approach a mountain they must either go around it or tunnel through it.

Tunnels were such a new idea in 1825 that engineers building them had to define them in their proposals. One proposal defined tunnels as "like a large well dug horizontally through a hill or mountain." Railroad companies began building tunnels in the mid-1830s. Today, tunnels are commonplace for both railroads and highways.

The first railways used stone blocks as a foundation to support the rails. An example of this kind of rail construction was revealed in an archaeological excavation in 1983 of a rail line built in 1811 between Gloucester and Cheltenham, England. The rails had been removed, but the stones remained. Each stone was about 1 foot (0.3 m) square, and stones were placed about 2 feet (0.6 m) apart.

Because the stones did not tie the two rails together they often shifted with weather variations, causing accidents. The solution to shifting rails was wooden **crossties,** *which connected the two rails. Rails are fastened to crossties with metal spikes, keeping them in place and keeping the rails at a constant distance from each other.*

As nineteenth-century railroad building accelerated, work teams stream-lined the track-laying process. One team prepared the road bed and laid the crossties. They were followed by another team who placed sections of rail on the crossties and positioned them so that train wheels precisely fit the rails. Another team drove the spikes that fastened the rails to the crossties.

Major roadways may have underpasses or overpasses to allow them to avoid railroad crossings. Crossings in remote areas may have only warning signs. Motorists at those crossings are responsible for checking for oncoming trains before crossing.

Early Safety Innovations

Injuries often occurred while workers were connecting one railcar to another using a "link and pin" connector. Workers had to line up the holes in the linking rods of both cars, then drop a pin through the holes to connect the

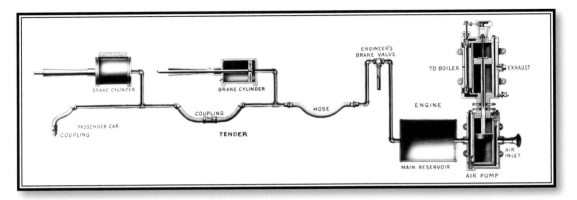

The Westinghouse air break replaced manually operated breaks. Compressed air was used to stop the trains.

cars. The invention of the *knuckle coupler* in 1868 by Eli Janney greatly reduced accidents while connecting railcars. The knuckle coupler was a semiautomatic device that dropped the connecting pin when the engineer backed the front car into the rear car. Workers no longer needed to stand between cars being connected or disconnected. A version of this coupler is still in use today.

As locomotives began to travel faster, better braking systems were needed. In 1869, George Westinghouse developed an *air brake* to replace manually operated mechanical brakes. Air brakes use compressed air to stop the train.

Inventions and innovations have evolved continuously since the first railroad was built in the early nineteenth century. Altogether, they make up today's high-speed modern railroad.

CHAPTER FIVE

The Railroad Era

After Robert Stephenson's Rocket was chosen in 1829 to run on the Liverpool to Manchester railway, the railway system in Britain expanded rapidly. Britain is a geographically small country with a mostly flat landscape, which is ideal for railway construction.

Trevithick's and the Stephensons' inventions soon crossed the Atlantic Ocean to the United States. The United States is a vast expanse of mountains, prairies, rivers, and coastlines. In 1829, most of its population lived along the coasts and in the states that had been the original thirteen colonies. The new railroad technology was just what was needed to connect distant communities isolated from each other by mountains and wilderness.

Early Railroads in the United States

The first railroad in the United States was built to haul granite from a quarry in Quincy, Massachusetts, to the Neponset River 3 miles (4.8 km) away. There it was loaded onto barges and floated to its destination. It was built in 1827.

The second, also built in 1827, was built to haul coal, like the earliest railroads in Britain. It ran from coal mines in Mauch Chunk, Pennsylvania, to the Lehigh River, a distance of 9 miles (14 km). Its rails were timber placed on wooden sleepers and reinforced with iron bars.

The earliest locomotive railroad in the United States that offered scheduled passenger service was the South Carolina Railroad and Canal Company. To build it, a group of Charleston investors met in 1827 to form the company. The locomotive made its first 6-mile (10-km) trip out of Charleston on Christmas day, 1830, carrying 141 passengers. The company completed its 136-mile (219-km) line from Charleston to Hamburg, South Carolina, in 1833.

The Baltimore and Ohio Railroad Company was also formed in 1827, and it made its first run of 1.5 miles (2.4 km) in 1829. That was a year before the South Carolina Railroad trip, but the first B&O train was horse-drawn. Its locomotive York started service in 1831.

In 1828, the Delaware and Hudson Canal Company built a railway from its coal mines in Honesdale, Pennsylvania, several miles to the newly built Delaware and Hudson Canal. In 1829, a steam locomotive, the Stourbridge Lion, was imported to Honesdale from Stourbridge, England, and became the first locomotive to run anywhere in North America.

Companies seeking funding for railroad expansion had to overcome competition from canal companies seeking funding. The first privately funded capital project in the United States of more than $1 million was the 100-mile (161-km) Delaware and Hudson Canal and its short railroad, which brought coal from Pennsylvania to New York City.

Once railroads proved to be profitable, investors were eager to provide funds for expansion, but the earliest railroads, without any track record of profitability, still had a hard time raising money.

The Camden and Amboy Railroad in

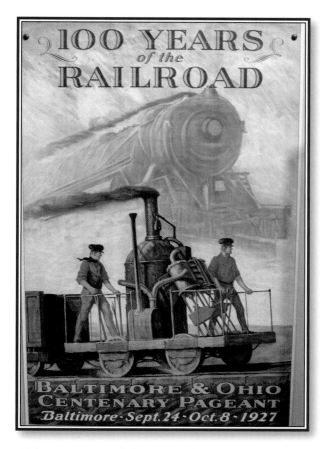

This poster celebrated the one-hundred-year anniversary of the Baltimore and Ohio railroad in 1927.

After raising funds for many years, the locomotive Johnny Bull made its first journey on the Camden & Amboy Railroad.

New Jersey was one of the first competitors for funding. Colonel John Stevens spent several years acquiring funding and a charter for his railroad to run from Camden to Amboy, New Jersey. His rail-travel line was started in 1831 and completed in 1834.

The advantages of rail soon became apparent. Railroads cut transit times tenfold and therefore reduced the cost of shipping goods, resulting in an acceleration of the U.S. economy before and after the Civil War. By the early 1840s, there were almost two hundred railroad projects either underway or completed. Most of these were in the eastern United States, the nation's population center in the early nineteenth century. These pioneering railroads demonstrated the superiority of rail transport.

Railroad tracks were easier and cheaper to build than

canals, and unlike waterways, railroads could be located wherever they were needed. Railroads were vastly superior to the wagons and coaches used to travel where there were no rivers or canals. That was very important in a country whose government wanted to encourage settlers to move west.

Westward Movement

By the mid-nineteenth century, the United States owned vast, but sparsely settled, territories west of the Mississippi. U.S. presidents and congressmen believed that the best way to protect these territories was for citizens to settle them and make them into states. Congress passed the Homestead Act, which granted land, free of charge, to settlers who would build a house and live on the land.

Congress also passed acts granting public land to railroads to encourage them to expand into sparsely settled areas. The railroad companies could sell the land to settlers and use the money to build more railroads. In 1830, there were only 23 miles (37 km) of railroad in the United States. By 1860, there were 30,000 miles (48,270 km) of railroad, mostly in the East.

Congress wanted a transcontinental railroad that reached the Pacific Ocean. To encourage the railroads, Congress passed the Pacific Railway Act of 1862 the same year it passed the Homestead Act. The act granted

Railroads were needed as more and more people emigrated to the west. The goal of Congress was to create a railroad that reached from the East Coast to the Pacific Ocean.

millions of acres of land to railroad companies willing to build a transcontinental railroad.

The Transcontinental Railroad

The Pacific Railway Act authorized the building of the transcontinental railroad. The Union Pacific Railroad would build west from Omaha, Nebraska, the farthest west the nation's existing rail network then extended. The Central Pacific Railroad would build east from Sacramento, California.

The act granted 33 million acres (13,365,000 hectares) to the railroad builders. The land would be used to establish towns and would be sold to settlers. The golden spike, which signified the meeting of the two railroads, was driven into a crosstie at Promontory Summit in Utah Territory in 1869. The nation was then joined from New York to California with 3,500 miles (5,632 km) of railroad operated by dozens of interconnected companies.

Settlers could then take the train to their homestead sites in the western territories. No longer did they need to travel for months through dangerous territory in rickety and unsafe prairie schooners. Settlement of the West increased rapidly. This population growth meant that territories could become states.

Building Railroads: Immigrant Labor

In the mid-nineteenth century, a famine in Ireland forced more than 1 million Irish people to flee to the United States. Many Irish laborers arrived in time to work on the great railroad expansion during the middle of the century. Many also worked to build New York's elevated railways. Irish immigrants supplied most of the labor for building the eastern section of the transcontinental railroad.

Chinese immigrants built the western section of the transcontinental railroad. Theirs was the harder task, because while most of the eastern portion of the railroad ran through flat prairie states, the western road had to climb mountains and bridge gorges before meeting its eastern counterpart at Promontory Summit.

The Irish immigrants who arrived in the United States during the potato famine suffered severe discrimination. They were often prevented from voting even after becoming citizens. They were forced to take the most menial jobs, which included laying railroad tracks.

Despite discrimination, Irish immigrants assimilated over time into the population. The Irish immigrants

Immigrants from Europe and Asia provided most of the labor for the great railroad expansion. In this illustration, Chinese immigrants work to build the Central Pacific Railroad.

shared similar ethnic roots with the American majority of that time and shared the language and many cultural similarities. The Chinese immigrants had a harder time. They were ethnically different from the American majority. The Chinese immigrants spoke different languages and had different religions and customs. These differences would enrich American culture, but as railroad work diminished, many Chinese people faced discrimination. Some helped establish the western agriculture industry, while others congregated in urban ghettos, or Chinatowns.

Industry Becomes Dependent on the Railroad

Railroads were an essential element in the development of western agriculture. They provided transportation to move produce from western states to eastern and midwestern markets. Midwestern and western states such as Nebraska and Iowa replaced eastern states such as Pennsylvania as the principal granaries of the nation. Many eastern lands that had been deforested in the eighteenth and nineteenth centuries to grow crops were allowed to return to forests, improving the ecosystem.

Other industries benefited from the growth of rail systems. Manufacturers could be located anywhere and use the railroads to bring in raw materials from far away and ship their finished goods throughout the country.

Railroad Magnates

Railroads created wealth for those who promoted and financed them. For example, four Sacramento businessmen joined together to create the Central Pacific Railroad company, which built the western section of the transcontinental railroad. They were Collis Huntington, Mark Hopkins, Leland Stanford, and Charles Crocker.

These four men also established other railroads, including the Southern Pacific Railroad, which ran from New Orleans through the Southwest to California. Because they controlled entire transportation routes, these and other railroad magnates, sometimes called robber barons for their ruthless business practices, could set high rates for travel and shipping.

High shipping rates especially hurt farmers wanting to ship their produce to market. In 1887, Congress passed the Interstate Commerce Act that began to lower rates through regulation of the industry.

Railroad Towns

In the same way that rivers and other waterways determined the location and size of early U.S. cities, the railroad similarly determined the fate of towns and cities established after the mid-nineteenth century. Towns and cities sprang up along railroad lines. However, their establishment and growth were not spontaneous.

Railroad companies worked to lure settlers to their territories.

The railroad companies left nothing to chance. They priced some land as low as two dollars per acre and provided buyers, frequently European immigrants, with generous credit terms. Prospective buyers were given low-cost round-trip tickets to view the land. Prospects were entertained along the way at "reception houses." Salesmen were never far away, always ready to close a sale.

The success of railroad towns varied. Some were well located, perhaps at the juncture of an east-west and a

Towns and cities were developed along railroad lines. Pictured is the city of Cumberland, Maryland on the Baltimore and Ohio Railroad.

north-south railroad, and prospered. Other successful towns attracted skilled businesspeople. However, many towns failed. Some may have been oversold by the railroad companies, and the promised growth failed to materialize. Settlers moved on to other towns, abandoning land and buildings. Some of these ghost towns can still be seen in remote parts of the western states. Other existing settlements became ghost towns because the railroads passed them by.

Railways Within Cities

While railroads were expanding throughout the country, large cities were developing a very different kind of railroad: rapid transit. Horse-drawn streetcars were one early form of intracity transportation. Streetcars were slow, even after they were electrified in the late nineteenth century.

Trains had been racing through the countryside at high

speeds for half a century by the time fast trains were introduced for intracity travel. For trains to speed through city streets unimpeded, they would have to travel on tracks elevated above the streets or else underground, beneath the streets. Underground railroads are called subways.

For a subway system to be built in Boston, the famous park, Boston Commons, had to be dug up.

Subways in the United States

The first subway in the United States was the Green Line in Boston, Massachusetts. Although it is a part of a light-rail, or trolley-car line, it began heading into downtown Boston via tunnel in 1897. Today, Boston has an extensive mass-transit system that uses both conventional subway trains and light-railcars that run on the surface and underground.

The largest subway system in the United States is New York City's. It began service in 1904 and has grown to include 722 miles (1,162 km) of track and 468 stations. Most people living in the crowded New York boroughs do not own cars. They depend on subways for transportation.

The Golden Age of Railroad Travel

From the late nineteenth century to the middle of the twentieth century, trains were preferred for long-distance travel. Trips could take as long as three or four days from coast to

Dining cars on trains were often as nice as 4-star restaurants. The dining car from the Northern Pacific Railway's North Coast Limited is pictured.

coast. Long-distance trains were often as luxurious as ocean liners. Travelers could have their own bedroom compartments, just as they would on a ship. Dining-car food and service were similar to that in fine restaurants.

Although it is still possible to travel around the country by train, few of the luxury trains remain. Some are still in service, operated as "cruise trains" on varying itineraries throughout the country at different times of the year. They are used by tourists who enjoy the scenery and the service and are not in a hurry. One cruise train is the luxurious

Many passengers reserve a stateroom when traveling on cruise trains. Pictured is a typical stateroom in a sleeping car.

American Orient Express, which has a varied itinerary, like a cruise ship. There are several others in the United States and in Canada.

Jet airline service, begun in the 1960s, has largely replaced trains for long-distance travel. Planes will never completely replace passenger trains, especially for short trips. Freight trains will continue to carry most of the heavy and bulky cargo, such as automobiles and building materials. In addition, railroad technology is being developed to allow high-speed train travel in the future. The golden age of railroads could return.

CHAPTER SIX

Railroads of the Future

By the 1960s, railroad passenger service was declining in popularity because of competition from airlines and automobiles. However, new high-speed rail technology also began developing at about the same time. This technology may someday reclaim some of the rail passengers and freight lost to the airlines and the interstate highway system.

Several high-speed, automated rail systems are in development. Some are very promising. The railway authority in France operates a high-speed train called Train à Gran Vitesse, or TGV, between Calais on the English Channel and Marseilles on the Mediterranean. It completes the 633-mile (1,018-km) journey in less than four hours. A passenger who has ridden the TGV reports, "When it passes another train on an adjacent track, the

This bullet train in Japan can travel at speeds of 177 miles (285 km) per hour. In highly populated cities, bullet trains can get passengers from one city to another faster than air travel.

'whosh sound' lasts less than two seconds, and when crossing an elevated trestle, looking down, the ground drops away so quickly it feels like a rocket taking off."

Japanese Bullet Trains

Bullet trains got their names because of the high speeds at which they travel. Bullet trains were introduced in Japan in 1964, but improvements to the technology are still being made. The newer model bullet train, which travels between Tokyo and Hakata, reaches speeds of 177 miles (285 km) per hour, which is actually 24 miles (15 km) per hour slower than the older trains. The speed has been reduced because of modifications that increase fuel efficiency and reduce noise. To reduce noise from air resistance, which is especially loud when entering tunnels, the train's nose has been shaped like a duck's bill. Taiwan is developing its own version of the bullet train. It has completed its first test run and will be put into service in October 2005. The trains, imported from Japan, will travel at speeds of up to 186 miles (299 km) per hour.

Fast trains are especially popular in Japan and some European countries because their high population densities limit the expansion of both automobile and air travel. In many cases, trains can travel from the center of one city to the center of another faster than passengers could make the trip by air.

Magnetic Levitation

An important rail technology still in the experimental stage is called *maglev,* or magnetic levitation. A maglev train rides on a cushion created by an electromagnetic reaction between an on board device and another embedded in the tracks. A maglev vehicle does not travel on existing rail-

The first Maglev train began regular service in 2004 in China. It can travel at speeds up to 270 miles (434 km) per hour.

road tracks. However, it could share the same infrastructure, including track right-of-way and passenger stations.

Japanese railway authorities have designed a project called the Linear Chuo Shinkansen Project, which will connect Tokyo and Osaka with a maglev train that reaches a speed of 310 miles (499 km) per hour. The authorities say, "The superconductive Maglev train, which levitates while traveling, makes the best use of the clean electrical energy. It has less noise and vibration, and minimizes the impact on the environment along its line."

Commercial Maglev Service

Engineers in Germany have been testing a maglev train, and while it has not been put into service in Germany, it has been adopted by China. The Chinese maglev connects the city of Shanghai with its airport some miles from the city. It is the world's first commercial, high-speed maglev service with full-size vehicles.

If the high-speed locomotives now in use in Japan and in Europe were to be used in the United States, existing railroad tracks would have to be modified. Some modification has been tried on tracks between New York City and Washington, D.C. Most modification involves eliminating even small irregularities in track construction and correcting the banking of curves.

Tilting Trains

A British company, Virgin Trains, is reviving a high-speed train project that was tried and abandoned two decades ago. These trains will eventually travel at 124 miles (200 km) per hour between London and Glasgow. When the trains go into curves at high speeds, they tilt to the right or left, depending on the direction of the curve. Tilting prevents passenger discomfort at high speeds; however, it was found that too much of a tilt made some passengers sick. It was discovered that reducing the amount of tilt allowed passengers to feel some of the effect of centrifugal force going through the curve, and that reduced the feelings of sickness. With that problem solved, the company plans to proceed with the project.

Travel Corridors

Regional rail authorities around the country, along with private transportation companies, are developing "travel corridors" to connect rail systems and eliminate traffic congestion.

Some examples of cities being connected with rail systems on the West Coast are Vancouver–Seattle–Portland; Oakland–East Bay–Sacramento; Los Angeles–San Diego. In the Midwest, rail lines radiate from Chicago to Minneapolis–St. Paul, to Milwaukee, to St. Louis, and to Detroit. The Amtrak line from New York to Washington, D.C., carries more passengers than either of the air shuttles that travel the route. By developing these strategically located travel corridors, passenger rail service may begin to recover some travel business it lost to the airline industry. In the future, passenger rail service could once again be commonplace between U.S. cities.

This travel corridor goes from Washington DC to Boston. The rail industry is hoping to recover travel business lost to airlines.

The Railroad: A Timeline

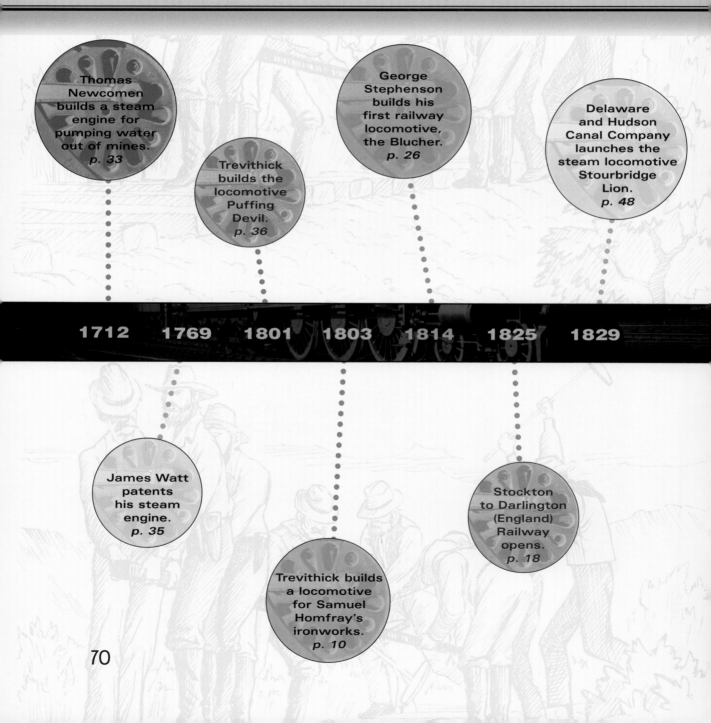

Thomas Newcomen builds a steam engine for pumping water out of mines.
p. 33

Trevithick builds the locomotive Puffing Devil.
p. 36

George Stephenson builds his first railway locomotive, the Blucher.
p. 26

Delaware and Hudson Canal Company launches the steam locomotive Stourbridge Lion.
p. 48

1712   1769   1801   1803   1814   1825   1829

James Watt patents his steam engine.
p. 35

Trevithick builds a locomotive for Samuel Homfray's ironworks.
p. 10

Stockton to Darlington (England) Railway opens.
p. 18

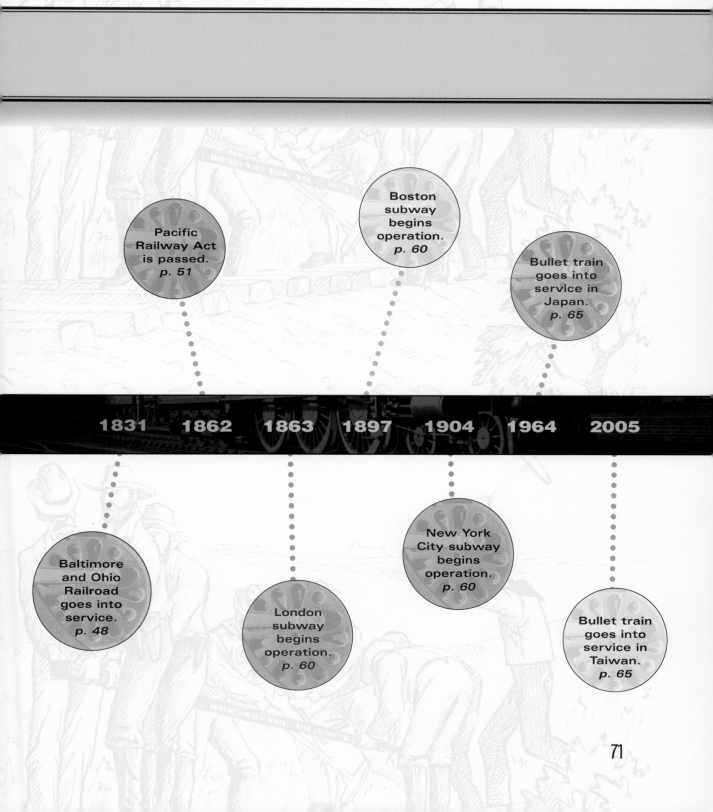

Pacific
Railway Act
is passed.
p. 51

Boston
subway
begins
operation.
p. 60

Bullet train
goes into
service in
Japan.
p. 65

1831　　1862　　1863　　1897　　1904　　1964　　2005

Baltimore
and Ohio
Railroad
goes into
service.
p. 48

London
subway
begins
operation.
p. 60

New York
City subway
begins
operation.
p. 60

Bullet train
goes into
service in
Taiwan.
p. 65

71

Glossary

air brake: a brake that uses compressed air to stop trains and other large vehicles

commuter train: a railway train that carries people from suburbs to a city center

condenser: a chamber in a steam engine that cools steam and turns it back into water

Conestoga wagon: a freight wagon, usually with a canvas cover and drawn by six horses

crossties: timbers laid horizontally underneath rails

engineer: a person who knew how to make and repair engines in eighteenth-century England; the person on trains who controls the locomotive *fireman:* the person on steam locomotives who shovels coal into the firebox; the person who stoked the firebox of any steam engine before the invention of the locomotive

flange: a lip on the inside edge of train wheels that keeps the wheels from slipping off the rail

knuckle coupler: a device for connecting railcars to each other

light rail: an urban transportation system using electric rail-cars, similar to subways and streetcars

locomotive: an engine that pulls railcars

maglev: magnetic levitation; a high-speed rail system that uses electromagnets to keep railcars locked onto the railway

prairie schooner: a wagon used by settlers moving westward in the early to mid-nineteenth century

rapid-transit system: an intracity transportation system using subways or light rails

steam-blast: a pipe for capturing steam exhaust on a steam engine *streetcar:* a self-propelled electric railcar for intracity travel, now mostly replaced by buses, subways, or light rails

subway: an intracity railway that travels in tunnels beneath city streets

T-rail: a rail shaped like an upside-down capital T seen in cross-section; all present-day rails are T-rails

vacuum: the absence of air; in Watt's steam engine, the airless space in the condenser after steam had been converted back into water

wagon trains: groups of nineteenth-century settlers traveling together, usually to western territories

wagonway: crude wooden rails for guiding coal wagons prior to the invention of the locomotive

To Find Out More

Books

Bain, David Haward. *Empire Express: Building the First Transcontinental Railroad.* New York: Penguin USA, 2000.

Brown, Dee. *Hear That Lonesome Whistle Blow: The Epic Story of the Transcontinental Railroads.* New York: Owl Books, 2001.

Link, O. Winston, and Thomas H. Garver. *The Last Steam Railroad in America.* New York: Harry Abrams, 2000.

Reynolds, Kirk, and Dave Oroszi. *Baltimore & Ohio Railroad.* Osceola, WI: Motorbooks International, 2002.

Rhodes, Michael. *North American Railyards,* 4th ed. Osceola, WI: Motorbooks International, 2003.

Walker, Pamela. *Train Rides.* Danbury, CT: Children's Press, 2000.

Web Sites

New York City Subway History

http://www.subwaywebnews.com/history.htm

This site contains a timeline, facts, and photos documenting subway history.

Railroad History

http://www.edsanders.com/railroad/history.htm

This is a multisubject Web site with many links to information about railroad history.

Smithsonian Transportation History

http://www.si.edu/resource/faq/nmah/transportation.htm

This page links to all Smithsonian sites relating to transportation.

Organizations

National Association of Railroad Passengers

900 2nd Street NE, Suite 308

Washington, DC 20002

Pennsylvania Railroad Technical & Historical Society

This membership organization publishes magazines, newsletters, and discussion forums.

Railway & Locomotive Historical Society

This membership organization promotes research, preserves documents, and has eight local chapters.

Index

About the Author

John R. Matthews is a freelance author living in Abilene, Texas. Matthews writes nonfiction books for both adults and children. He has a master's degree in history from Tarleton State University, part of the Texas A&M system. Matthews has loved trains since childhood. He vividly remembers traveling as a child from Texas to Florida in the 1950s in a luxurious train with private rooms and a superb restaurant car.

To research this book, Matthews read many books about trains as well as numerous articles from encyclopedias. A great number of Internet sites are devoted to the subject of trains. Matthews is looking forward to the day when he can once again travel to Florida on a luxurious train.